Forest Books

Through the Needle's Eye

**Jon Milos** was born in Stutjeska, Yugoslavia, of Romanian parents on 16 February 1930. He studied philosophy at the University of Belgrade (1950–1955) and attained a degree in linguistics at the Sorbonne (1960–1963). He also studied at Ecole des Hautes Etudes in Paris (1963–1964). Working as a linguist, he has lived in Sweden since 1964.

Considered unique in his skills by important writers in Sweden, Yugoslavia and Romania, Jon Milos has written twelve books of poetry, seven in Romanian, three in Serbo/ Croatian, and two in Swedish. As a translator into Romanian, Swedish, Macedonian and French, he received the Artur Lundkvist Serbo/Croatian prize in 1978. To date has has published thirty-two books, and is a member of the Swedish and Yugoslavian Writers' unions.

**Brenda Walker**'s career has been divided between the arts and education, her university studies being at London and Keele. During the last few years she has devoted herself to poetry in translation, working on Romanian, Urdu and Hindi texts. Her own poetry is published by Headland Press.

*Jon Milos*

# *Through the Needle's Eye*

**FOREST
BOOKS**
*London & Boston*

Poems
by **Jon
MILOS**

*Translated from
the Romanian &
the Swedish by*
**Brenda Walker**

U.S. DISTRIBUTOR
**DUFOUR EDITIONS**
CHESTER SPRINGS,
PA 19425-0449
(215) 458-5005

PUBLISHED BY
FOREST BOOKS
20 Forest View, Chingford, London, E4 7AY, U.K.
61 Lincoln Road, Wayland, MA 01778, U.S.A

Typeset in Great Britain by Cover to Cover, Cambridge
Printed in Great Britain by BPCC Wheatons Ltd, Exeter

First Published 1990

*British Library Cataloguing in Publication Data*
Milos, Jon
Through the needle's eye: poems of Jon Milos.
I. Poetry in Romanian 1945 — English texts
I.  Title    II.   Walker, Brenda, 1934
859'.134

*Library of Congress catalog Card No*
89–83342

Forest Books gratefully acknowledge the support of
the Swedish Institute

# Contents

Introduction by Brenda Walker ix
In four languages xii
Don't say anything xiii
My world xv

On Red Carpet Roads
On red carpet roads 2
I am for wild beasts 3
In secret hands 4
Progress 5
Death is guilty 6
Simple and efficient 7
Nobody can fight against fate 8
Smart and optimistic 9
So far 10
Meeting 11
People 12
Sweet smiles 13
All is perfect 14
Don't show yourself 15
Bulls and snails 16
God's powerlessness 17
Die 18

A Water Party
A water party 20
The beautiful people 21
Sit on two chairs 22
Dreams 23
Holiday 24
Why do people need 25
Green thoughts 26
Definitions 27
Truth 28
The lie 28

The bureaucrat 28
Ten points of view 29
Watch out for people 30

LOVE WITH AUXILIARY HEAT
Warm love 32
My love and your love 33
The angelic woman 34
Loneliness 35
It's cold in bed 36
Solitary people 37
A dialogue 38
A new female world 39
Love is not a myth anymore 40
Forgive 41
Words 42
People meet 43
Divorce 44
Love — play 45
Don't ask me 46
Love 47
Hate 48

THE WOLF DOESN'T FRIGHTEN CHILDREN ANYMORE
The world doesn't frighten children anymore 50
On earth as it is in heaven 51
Civilisation 52
I am thinking of human beings 53
Flowers and people 54
Unbuilt violin 55
Pegasus 56

DON'T STAY OUTSIDE
Raise your finger 58
Don't stay outside 59
Migrant workers 60
Tomorrow 61
In the best of worlds 62
The future 63
From today 64

The dwarf from the summer garden    65
Si vis pacem para bellum    66
The forest    67
In Moscow as in Washington    68
The snake and the spider    69
The churchyard    71
Life after death    72

STAY IN YOUR OWN SKIN
Careful    74
Poetry    75
Retraining    76
Repetitio mater studiorum est    77
Thought and heart    78
Nothing is changed    79
History    80
Poet    81
Stay in your own skin    82
The yellow pain of the day    83
Summer    84
To be is to laugh    85
Go there    86
Emptiness    87
Birds    88
There are days    89
Love    90
Happiness    91
Love and future    92
Poesia non muori    93

# Acknowledgements

These poems have been selected from the following volumes:

*The Everlasting Dawn*, 1977 Romania
*Bulls and Snails*, 1982 Romania
*Borealis Wedding*, 1984 Romania
*Water Party* 1985 Romania
*Eggs Without Shells*, 1986 Romania
*The Seed*, 1978 Sweden
*In Four Languages*, 1990 Sweden
*Seeds*, 1981 Yugoslavia
*From Day to Day*, 1986 Yugoslavia
*So Die Thoughts and Time*, 1988 Yugoslavia

# Introduction:
## *In Four Languages*

Recently Jon Milos published in Swedish a thick volume of poetry, commended by critics, with the title *In Four Languages*. It contains poems from different periods written in Romanian, Serbo-Croatian, Swedish and French. Jon Milos was born of Romanian parents in Yugoslavia, but after University studies in Belgrade and Paris, he went to live in Sweden. He has written ten collections of poetry in Romanian, Serbo-Croatian or Swedish. Also an industrious translator, he has introduced several Swedish authors to Romania and Yugoslavia, and vice versa. Besides individual authors, he has edited and translated anthologies of poetry and prose from these three countries. He also translates from the French.

Many Swedish critics have acclaimed his works. Tommy Olofsson describes Milos as a chameleon not only in his poetry but also in linguistics, for his work has great variety. 'High-sounding, rhetorically lavish poems, sometimes spiced with learned allusions or Latin quotations, are included among "indignation poems", naivistic flourishes and ironically turned maxims.' Lars Nygren speaks of him as a poet with 'a warm masculine temperament who has much at heart.' He finds his poetry full-blooded because of the sensual ardour Milos conveys when writing about women and love, in a stoic or reflective melancholy, always conscious of love's price:

> *Only the dead*
> *Make love to each other free of charge.*

Some of the poems are concerned with great existential questions about death, love and life. He is a philosopher who considers man's stupidity, his vanity, his inability to communicate as a social being, and the absence of God. His poems are a protest against man alone in a cynical world, and against the degradation of man and nature. He sees man as part of this physical cycle and celebrates it in his work. Yet he rages against oppression. Ulf Malmqvist speaks of Milos's 'engaged and reflective poetry which constantly upholds man's inborn dignity in a world in which human worth is neglected.'

His poetry is peopled with beings who appear larger than in life and so the reader is easily captured. One can find terse matter-of-fact comments or those that are deeply profound. He can be extravagant with words one minute but sparing the next, lyrically reflective or coldly satirical. His metrical structure is free and the tone often colloquial. His aphorisms are tight and thought-provoking, and it is here where Malmqvist finds him at his best. He chooses 'Pegasus' as a fine example where Milos demonstrates 'in an exquisite way, the poetic vein that he definitely possesses':

> *Only Pegasus*
> *Can stop the horses of the Apocalypse*
> *Let him fly!*

In Romania the well-known critic Serban Cioculescu considered him an innovator of the Romanian language who showed striking originality. Several of the poems in this volume ring of compassion, and, with deep understanding, Milos sounds the state of things in a world that for a long time has experienced the rise and fall of ideologies. Yet he does not always look on the dark side and never loses his sense of humour. 'To be is to laugh', he writes in one poem, 'in a world like ours/in death-throes.' It is not by accident that Milos writes about poetry ('Pegasus', 'Poesia non muori', 'Poetry'). He considers it our only chance of salvation. He once recalled that when famous tennis players compete, they attract a great crowd despite the cost of the tickets, the same applying to well-known pop stars. However, when great poets read at literary events it is rare in most countries for them to have large audiencies, even though tickets might be free. Yet he feels poetry is the best way of defending ourselves from artificial culture and from cold shadows in our hearts.

The eternal curse of exile is forever with Milos, for in Yugoslavia he is not Yugoslavian, in Romania not Romanian and in Sweden not Swedish, and despite the fact that great critics in all three countries view his originality as a gift, some comparing him to a prism, the core of his style remains ironical, and sometimes against himself. Many famous authors have chosen to switch to a different language, but usually the successful ones have been authors of prose. A poet faces a much harder task and therefore his fate is the tragic fate of Ovid. Yet Jon Milos has never switched languages, he just chose to write in all four, which makes him unique in the history of literature.

He has always viewed the nationalistic element of one culture, one language, as limiting, and so set out to learn not only the grammar of a new tongue, but also the prevailing cultural rules and structures, so he could think and feel according to those norms. By having embraced several cultures he sees himself as richer, both as a being, and as a writer. Overriding the deep feeling of exile he writes:

> *To possess several cultures and to speak several languages does not mean loss of identity, but rather a strengthening of it.*

Brenda Walker
*London*

# In four languages

I come to the well
Crying with a flower in my hand
No longer can I see my picture in the water
I come from love
People do not recognise me
My skin is blue from snake bites.
I have remained a child
I speak words naked
In four languages
One can see who I am
But in none am I understood.

In Yugoslavia not Yugoslav
In Sweden not Swede
In France not French
In Romania a foreigner.

A wagtail scolds me
Because of a rose
A worm spits at me
Because of a daisy
Cyclops hit me
Because I am not one-eyed
Bloodhounds cannot smell me
They bark, bark, bark . . .

I am not allowed to be an eagle
With azure wings
Nor to participate in the festivities of the mind.

I am entitled to silence
Sleeping pills and work
To raise others to the light.

# Don't say anything

Don't say anything to the angels
About freedom
They might believe you
And lose their vision of the world

Freedom is the only illusion
That is punished

Don't say anything to the dead
About resurrection
They might believe you
And try to rise from the dead

The dead believe everything you say.

# What happiness

What happiness
To live in this happy world!

Science teaches us to think like gods
How many vitamins to swallow
How many hours to sleep
How to live and die healthy.

The State defends us
Against neighbours and other beasts
Teaches us to make money and children.

Politics cleans our brains
From the larvae of divergent ideas
Teaches us to act and choose correctly
No clouds or oysters in our memories.

The Church blesses us
Protects our souls from evil spirits
Shows us the way to heaven.

# My world

My world
Is not the world of optimists
Blind, happy with indifference
No sorrow can make them suffer
Hearts separated from conscience
Run laughing in the streets
They chase the sun setting with time
Cut down trees in the blood
Fill water with dead birds
They sow winds over the world
Proudly singing as they drink
While nature
Dies of poverty and poison
The pessimists are the creators
With a microscope in the brain
They see the unseen
They make the desert flower
Lead us to life and light
To baptism in the far dawn.

# 1

# *On* $R$*ed* $C$*arpet* $R$*oads*

# On red carpet roads

Children have nowhere to play
Snakes are set free in the park
Thieves adorned with medals
Celebrated like Olympic victors
The telephone rings — no police answer
The policemen are having coffee
While the dogs nibble sugar lumps
And play cards with laws
Cold spirits shape our lives
The Law sweeps the streets with morals
Morals sell old buttons at the flea-market
Truth is objectively asleep

No one any longer says — I am human
It doesn't pay

On red carpet roads
Only crayfish walk forward.

# I am for wild beasts

Tame animals don't interest me
I am for wild beasts
The origin of man is wolf
Not ape
Homo homini lupus est.
In the jungle everything can grow
On asphalt nothing grows
If they were able to see with them
Bulls' horns would not be so hard.
Destroy — and the world will remember you!
Raise yourself up and laugh from up there
Over plains of swaying reeds.

# In secure hands

Politics has taken over fate
And comforts the world with illusions
Bureaucrats, technocrats, psychocrats
Squeeze light out of the water
And teach fish how to swim
Professors crammed with learning
Cure children from laughter and imagination
And chase reason into the shadows
Specialists on words and figures
Paint rainbows in offices
Lock truth in the desk drawer
And take the lift up to heaven
Theocrats frighten people with the end of the world
Death is praised in the name of God
Don Juan-patriots and music-hall stars
Drink roses on the moon
And cover reality with snow-flakes
Problems are transformed into foam
Today only hawkers know what culture is
Life is in secure hands.

## Progress

When eating the forbidden fruit
Adam lost Paradise
But thus created the world

When stealing the fire
Prometheus lost heaven
But thus gave light to the world

When killing his brother
Cain improved his standard of living

# Death is guilty

I have a pen in my hand
Instead of a gun
And am thinking:
There's nothing easier
Than killing a man
One shot — and it's over.
I am not guilty
You are not guilty
Nobody's guilty
The pen is frightened and silent
Death is guilty.

# Simple and efficient

People as human beings
Don't interest me
I prefer the concrete and social person
A man who can produce
Useful matters and things
Pots, plastic roses and golf balls
Organised beings
Not dreamers and idealists
Who intoxicate reality with words
And turn life upside down
The future is technique, economy and defence.
They'll improve life
And save us from death.
Thus: four plus four make eight
Eight multiplied by eight is sixtyfour already
Paradise is built this way:
With simplicity, logic and efficiency.

# Nobody can fight against fate

Why shouldn't I lie
Everyone else does
Why shouldn't I steal
When everyone else steals
I am not Job
Lying with faith on the refuse dump
Nor Jesus
Dying on the cross
Nor Socrates
Drinking poison from the cup
Nor Giordano Bruno
Letting myself be burned alive
Whetting lenses like Spinoza
Nobody can fight against fate
Money sings in the light
In the dark poverty laments
God bleeds with loneliness in heaven
The lawyers are on holiday
Playing poker with the dolphins.

# Smart and optimistic

Be a respectful citizen
Don't provoke the gods
Love your country like yourself
Take public opinion into consideration
Understand politics correctly
Don't seek the needle in the haystack
Be happy about your pay rise
About your purchasing power
Build up happiness
Don't disturb truth
Believe in wonders
Drink beer dance the bird dance
Be smart and optimistic
In this way you will save
Your head from darkness
And conquer the air.

# So far

So far no one has complained
About lack of intelligence
And no one has gone to school to learn
To be a human being
Everyone thinks he was born one.

Once people went to the market-place
To watch stupidity
Now they stay home
And watch it on TV — in colour.

# Meetings

From the market-place that smells of gunpowder
One can hear:
Life would be so much more beautiful
If it resembled children's dreams
We should see things with new eyes
love women with fresh feelings
Those who don't understand the spirit of today
Should disappear from History.

Then another speaker came
to talk about the metaphysics of hens:

We should let hens stay as hens
Make love to the cocks
And lay eggs
Only then will they be happy
And give us offspring handsome and wise.

Nonsense, cried a cock in a stand
You can't make me drunk on cold water
He did three somersaults
And changed into a bomb.

The market-place exploded with applause.

# People

People on the right, people on the left.
Homo sapiens. Homo lupus. Homo consumens.
Superman. The new man.
The cosmic man.
A man who laughs
A man who cries
A man who murders
In the name of freedom
In the name of peace.
People building chimeras
Who produce happiness
Who improve our standard of living
Who sow monuments in churchyards
In the name of love.
From person to person
Multiplied people, divided people
From heart to heart
From race to race
From throne to throne
From gold to gold.
On the right. On the left.
But how can we recognise a human being
When so many carry knives in their hands?

## Sweet smiles

The eagles no longer attack rats
Now they chase people
Squirrels aim nuts at children's heads
Behind every leaf a microphone is hidden
Secret agents
Dig like moles into your soul
Restaurants are full of hearts
Drowning in their glasses
Lovers have only their bed in common
Ideas flee from lice and police
Sweet smiles
Throw knives at your back
Barbarity's smiling humanism

I am alone like the moon
Over dark endless waters
Oh God
The strong ones are the first to give up.

# All is perfect

All is perfect and in order
The standard of living increases
The stars talk to each other on the phone
People are dressed as objects
Complete identification between things and beings
Coloured women nurse and bathe white children
White children lie in the sun to become brown
Ideas fondle the hens at the pond
Equality is solidarity: the frogs want to be cows
The moles are learning to fly
The swans make love to tom cats in the park
The flowers have only one wish:
To be flowers and to flower.

Only the working-day is longer than it should be
People have no time to live any more
They commit suicide
The objects watch surprised.

The tax on profit tells its own story . . .

# Don't show yourself

Tear leaves in the wind
Beat water in the mortar
Let others solve the problems

Bewitch existence
Beautify truth
Reality will then look more real

Wrap up in words
Don't show yourself

Great is he
Who is invisible.

# Bulls and snails

Why can't bulls see with the ends of their horns
Like snails
Since they were created with horns?

Why don't snails butt with their horns?
Like bulls
Since they were born with horns?

Why don't bulls withdraw inside themselves
Like snails
When we caress their soft muzzles?

Why don't bulls leave a trace
Like snails
When enchanted they encounter the sun?

# God's powerlessness

God lies abandoned on a bare mountain in Heaven
The Devil rules the world
God sits alone at table
Counting his ribs

The Devil builds monuments of victory
Blows fanfares
Dances in Parliament

God watches surprised how the spring water turns rusty
As he bleeds from loneliness
So far no woman wants to marry him
And no devil has been crucified

# Die

Die for truth
Die for freedom
Die for love

Die for God
Die for happiness
Die for your country

Die for money
Die for peace
Die for poetry
Die for an idea
Die for a flower
Die for a chair

Die for anything at all
But die
Die
Die
Die
Those who don't die
Will never rise again from the dead

# 2

# *A* *W*ater *P*arty

# A water party

I was invited to a water party
And was offered all kinds of drinks:
Mineral water, distilled water, rain water,
Cocacola, whisky, beer, wine, vodka, gin,
Sweet water, salt water, heavy water . . .
Drinking-water was the only thing I wasn't offered
Scientific waters guarantee life and health
The drinkable future
After a few hours I felt sick with thirst
And went home polluted and drunk.

# The beautiful people

I watch colour TV
The American film series
Dallas.

Bank account culture

Life with a glass in your hand
Instead of a book.

Beautiful people.

Business feeding on grass
With the cattle
Giving birth to money.

Unhappy souls at the psychiatrist's
Waiting to go through the needle's eye
To paradise.

# Sit on two chairs

Sit on two chairs
Carefully so you don't
Fall between them
And let the chairs quarrel
About which one you belong to.

Hunt two hares at the same time
Don't complain if you miss them.

You were allowed to feel the ground
And breathe fresh air.

# Dreams

If you dream that you find money
It means
That you'll also lose the money you've got
Don't take it!

If you dream that you are a flower
It means
That you'll have trouble with bees and butterflies
Be yourself!

If you dream that you die and can't be reborn
It means
That you've solved the problem of your life space
And will dream no more.

# Holiday

On the beaches of the world
People are asleep
Bellies to the sun

The sea is singing
Thought is dying
Salt drips from the nerves

Bought happiness

# Why do people need

Why do people need a head?
That is where the rot starts.

Why do people need a language?
The bird is caught because of its own singing.

Why do people need a nose?
They cannot smell their own stupidity.

Why do people need a heart?
It beats and beats then suddenly stops.

# Green thoughts

Don't strike the stone
The stone won't change

Don't frighten the shadows
Shadows cannot flee

Don't throw gold seeds to the hens
They are dreaming of maize.

# Definitions

Individualism = subject without predicate  
Plagiarism = loan without receipt  
Smile = wailing that cannot be heard  
Life = an image of water in an image of air  
Progress = measurement without measure  
Loneliness = a full stop left by words.  
Happiness = snowflake of nothingness.

# Truth

Truth is a fruit
That ripens in an abyss
In the garden only the lie ripens

# The lie

This face is the face of other faces
This face is the face of other faces
This face is the face of other faces

# The bureaucrat

When the bureaucrat leaves
He lets his shadow
Look after his desk.

# Ten points of view

God:
Believe that I exist — and I exist
Happy are those who do not see me

The snake:
Take a bite of the apple
And you will find truth

Prometheus:
Steal
And there will be light

Odysseus:
Wander
And you will find the place

Socrates:
Drink the poison
And leave the lie in the cup

Spartacus:
Wake the dragon
And freedom will sing

The woman:
Why don't oxes make love?
Why don't bulls work?

Don Juan:
Be cunning
Without bait you will catch no fish

Jesus:
Do good deeds
And you will be crucified

The Devil:
If only women remain women
All is well.

# Watch out for people

Watch out for people
Who never read a book
But believe they know everything
Anything could pop into their heads

Watch out for people
With eyes close to their hearts
They see only what they feel
And speak their minds

Watch out for people
Who take your place when you leave
Their faces are visible only in the dark
Illuminated by a strong wind

Watch out for people
Looking for human beings with a lantern in daylight
They cannot see the mote and the beam
But shine like the moon with the light of others.

# 3

## *L*ove
## *W*ith
## *A*uxiliary
## *H*eat

# Warm love

Love does not exist in Sweden
Said a Swedish girl to me
It is too cold

Love has need of heat
Lots of heat

So she journeys each summer
To another place in search of warmth

And she dreams . . .
And dreams

When she rouses
Love is nowhere to be found

Then she thinks . . .
And thinks

Love is like water
In heat it evaporates
In cold it freezes

# My love and your love

My love and your love
Love each other so much
That they no longer see anything.

My love and your love
See each other
And can love no more.

My love and your love
Hate each other so much
That they no longer see anything.

# The angelic woman

Beware of the angelic woman
She builds her nest in your heart
And will never leave
Until she has conquered all your roots
Until you can love no more
And nobody loves you
But no woman
Respects a slave
She gives you a deadly blow
And leaves you alone with your life
A woman is there to be loved
Not to be understood
Said Eve with a laugh
Before eating the forbidden fruit.

# Loneliness

You love your wife, children, your country.
You work. Earn money.
So die thoughts and time
Stallions become good-natured workhorses
And bulls rich oxes.

You buy things and dreams
Years pass over you like clouds.
Beautiful. Wonderful.

Suddenly
The apple begins to rot
And the wind to blow . . .

You daren't look back
You see nothing in front of you
Empty nests all around you
You hear the wolves of despair howling —
To possess everything and be nobody.

# It's cold in bed

It's cold in bed

My darling
Sits up counting money.

It is winter when people
No longer find time
To talk to each other
And make love.

When loneliness is stronger than words
Nightfly with scorched wings in your heart
Icy shadows rising in your dreams.

Keep the water running, darling
To wash away the spider webs of our feelings.

# Solitary people

Night
Empty streets
Houses in uniform
Solitary people
Sleep in front of the TV
A shadow is walking his dog
Money shines instead of street-lamps
An unwelcome intruder
Seeks the road to happiness
Stars quarrel with the owls
Loneliness knocks on the window
Restaurant doors
Open and close like mouths
The heart wants to dance
The body wants to sleep
Tomorrow is another working-day.

# A dialogue

— If you could choose
Between love and life
Which would you choose?

— Love.

— But how can you love me
If you no longer exist?
With your soul?

# A new female world

Men
Do not turn their heads after women any more
Women
Of today make men lose their heads
In the name of the categoric imperative
Of sexual liberation

A new female world

Without contradictions or opposition
With wolves as sweet as dolls
Where flowers grow from the problems
And people grow old with happiness
They love —
Instead of fighting.

# Love is not a myth anymore

I don't like Platonic love
It is like distilled water
Tasteless and undrinkable.

A real man
Proves himself in bed
Not at the summit of the Himalayas.

Only impotent people
Play the part of priests and philosophers.
The penis cannot read.

Seventy per cent of the wealth of the United States
Is in the hands of women
Fortunes acquired with love.

Love is not a myth any more.

Only the dead
Make love to each other free of charge.

# Forgive

Forgive the man
Who breaks his wife's nose
Forgive the woman
Who eats her husband's heart
Forgive your enemy
As the apple forgives the worm
Forgive death
As ashes forgive the wind
Forgive also God
Who does not forgive us.

# Words

Words, words. Only words.
Meaningless dogmas
Icy thoughts and foam.
It is cold among the words.
Love
Sleeps among snakes.

# People meet

People meet
Fall in love
Marry
Have children
Get fed up
Meet somebody else
And divorce
Children grow up
Fall in love
Marry
Have children
Get fed up
Meet somebody else
And divorce
Thus humanity increases
Day after day.

# Divorce

Get out — bloody poet!
I have fallen in love with someone else
I flourish
The kids are mine
You don't need money
You don't drive.

Fly to the eagles
Eat vitamins
Write poetry
Marry Poetry
Don't forget family maintenance
Love — is expensive.

# Love — play

When a woman makes love
She leans back
To give an impression
That she is defending herself.

When a man makes love
He bends down
To give an impression
That he is praying.

So begins
The hide-and-seek of love
The sexual whirlwind
Life that refuses to die.

# Don't ask me

Don't ask me
Who won the first Marathon
I am not interested in sport

Don't ask me
Who dropped the first nuclear bomb
That is not my problem

Don't ask me
Who painted the Mona Lisa
I don't care for Art

Don't ask me
Who got the Nobel prize in literature this year
I am not paid for that

Don't ask me
Who wrote the ninth sympony
Music doesn't move me.

Don't ask me
Who first set foot on the moon
I couldn't care less.

Don't ask me
Who murdered Julius Caesar
It is no concern of mine

Don't ask me
I have no time for stupid things
I have my job to do
And my family to care for
About anything else
I don't give a damn.

# Love

*A linguist*
   Love is a beautiful noun
   Instead of an ugly verb.

*A philosopher*
   From the outside come those looking for love
   Love comes from inside.

*An electrician*
   Love is like electricity
   Connect the plug and there is light.

*A farmer*
   Love is like dew
   It comes from nowhere and disappears the same way.

*An accountant*
   Love is the only loss
   To give the impression of profit.

*A poet*
   As long as there is love
   There is also poetry.
   When love disappears
   Critique begins.

*A pedagogue*
   Most people are unable to love
   Only they are brought up to it.

*An old man*
   Anybody who once burnt himself on love
   Will light the fire no more
   He will rebuild his life from the ashes.

*A barman*
   The glass of love is there to drink
   Not to be filled with cathedral and moonlight.

*A lawyer*
   Those who do not love
   Will escape unfaithfulness.

# Hate

Nothing hurts your soul
More than hate
That is why there are so many invalids.

# 4

## The Wolf Doesn't Frighten Children Anymore

# The wolf doesn't frighten
children any more

The wolf doesn't frighten children any more
Now the psychiatrist and the 'ombudsman'
Will teach them to live as they have to
In accordance with the constitution of a consumer society
It is not a question of being anybody
The most important thing is to exist
To play tennis every morning
Between seven and eight
To love Status Quo and the flag
To believe that snails have wings
And that one plus one
Equals absolutely anything.

A dog barks in the classroom:
I bite anyone
Who doesn't think and calculate correctly.

# On earth as it is in heaven

One day
If science is allowed to decide
All children
Will be born like Jesus
By the Virgin and the Holy Spirit
In a test tube.
Grow up at the day-nursery —
According to statistics —
Without feelings or sensations
Eat sweets together with their toys
And talk to the video.

The boys will look like girls
The girls like boys
And they'll all look the same
Like angels.

On earth as it is in heaven.

# Civilisation

Mothers no longer have time to be mothers
Dozing sleepily in the office
Typing their lives into word processors.
Babies drink milk from bottles
And see the world through glass.

In schools ethics is no longer taught
But sex technique and marketing
Industrial pedagogy of reality
Moral laziness
Musical sleep
You nod your head — you agree
You shrug you shoulders — none of your business
An attractive smile — you don't understand
No leaf is like another leaf
But they're all called — leaves
And you no longer know
What is life
Or what is dream.

A parrot repeats:
This you can do
This you can't
This you can do
This you can't.

# I am thinking of human beings

I am thinking of human beings
And take an axe in my hand
Humans are the only creatures
Who kill the ones they love
Who swear love and friendship
But then betray and destroy
Lustfully harming others
Killing with joy
Animals never desert their young
Unprepared for life
Nor do the birds
Before their young can fly
Only humans beat their children
Divorce and disappear . . .

# Flowers and people

Flowers are wiser than people
They don't boast about their beauty and scent
They blossom because they are flowers
And don't care about the gardener's plans

Flowers are wiser than people
They don't worship godlike images
They believe in their flowering
And don't care about howling winds

# Unbuilt violin

It was love
That brought me to Sweden
I sacrificed poetry
For the happiness in things
The horizon — for a secure existence
There is no happiness
Up there with the eagles
All that exists
Grows from the earth — from below
From above
One can only fall down
I was no longer interested in
Socrates and the categorical imperative
Who thinks of the spring
When swimming in the sea
My truth was love
That ontological wound
The flower of intoxication in the blood
Thus began my conflict with fate
The fall in the mirror
And the tree remained a tree
Unbuilt violin.

# Pegasus

Only Pegasus
Can stop the horses of the Apocalypse
Let him fly!

# 5

# *D*on't
# *S*tay
# *O*utside

# Raise your finger

Raise your finger
Feel the direction of the wind
Choose the proper way
And go forward.

Loneliness is not for people.

Don't be afraid of dragons
Evil spirits
Or sirens

God is with you.

Don't worry about
Buried chrysanthemums.

When you arrive
Angels will be waiting
With flags in their hands.

## Don't stay outside

Don't stay outside
When the musicians play
And dancing rings are spreading
Join the ring and dance

Live for other people and die

Thus you conquer egotism
And middleclass feeling
Thus the caterpiller becomes
A butterfly with azur wings

A soul with the heart in its hand.

# Migrant workers

In welfare cities
Migrant workers worn out by injustice
Souls as lonely as loneliness
Excluded from life and language
As if they weren't human
As if they were nothing.

# Tomorrow

Capitalism refuses to die
Shining on unknown winds.

Socialism cannot find the road
Playing heroic marches.

Stones do not embrace
Tomorrow with dandelions in the windows.

# In the best of worlds

In the best of worlds
Welfare admires itself in the mirror
Throwing thoughts into the pond.
Life puts pebbles in coffee cups
And people drink it happily
Fragrant
Illusion is transformed to reality.
Freedom
Parades in the streets in police cars
Crosses flower in the churchyards
Happy are those who keep quiet.
A cricket sings to the moon
Above the clouds the sky is always blue:
What you can't see does not exist
What you can't see does not exist.

# The future

One day
Just as one can read in the prospectus
Everyone will be free and rich
The night
Will fall to the left and right of time
The red thread of dreams
Will marry fire and water
Flames of happiness
Dancing from the heart.

Each and everyone
Will give what they can
And receive all they need
Happiness will fill the air
With cherry flowers
No forbidden fruit in the garden
All that exists will last and sing
Milk and honey
For all who believe and abide.

# From today

From today
Cats are no longer allowed to hunt mice
Now it is the turn of the mice to chase the cats.

From today
People can no longer give their lives
For truth
Now it is the turn of truth
To die for the people.

From today
The souls of geniuses
Are no longer allowed to be like mountain tops:
White and cold
Now they must be like those of the common people:
Red and warm.

From today
Wild and tame animals
Will caress each other like brothers and sisters
And sing Hosanna.

# The dwarf from the summer garden

The night is dense like a stone
Words flee from the owls
Life dies
The wolves howl
Madness is singing in the trees
The dwarf from the summer garden
Waters the stars
To be human
Is no longer allowed
The wind is asking:
Why?
Why?
Why?

## Si vis pacem
## para bellum

All is beautiful and fine
People wash their faces with light
Love defiles the streets with weapons in its hands
SI VIS PACEM PARA BELLUM
Only life
Is thinner, darker, smaller
Death is hungry
And eats with ruthless greed
Otherwise all is beautiful and fine
People wash their faces with light
Love defiles the streets with weapons in its hands
SI VIS PACEM PARA BELLUM
One day
There will be no wars any more
In the churchyards stalagmites of flowers
The necrofile historic Ark
Will carry humanity to the Other World
And all will be beautiful and fine.

## The forest

The forest can't see its own trees
The trees breathe helplessly in darkness
Sighs are heard from the garden
It is the snails who could not become bulls
Conquered philosophers
Measuring intelligence by profit
The metaphysical pole is rotting
A few fists beat the earth
The worms want to rise
A fruitless rosy kingdom
Perfumed bouquet of attitudes
Oh conscience, still waters,
How can I flee
How can I defend myself
From this eternity of fear?

# In Moscow as in Washington

*To Joseph Brodsky*

In Moscow as in Washington
Humanistic ideas hold people's hands
Promising welfare and peace
Happy oranges and golden roses
But so far no promise has come true
Neither in Moscow nor in Washington.

In Moscow as in Washington
Workers no longer fight for freedom
Now they demand comfort and happineses
Every evening they return dead
Yet believe that they're alive
As every morning
They rise up again and go to work
With the historical inevitability
On their lips.

In Moscow as in Washington
People sleep with fear under their pillows
They believe in love and future
God whines and weeps
The devil brags about his fame and laughs
Those who have money have everything
Their names inscribed on their foreheads
With power in their pockets.

Oh poets, fleas on the moon!
So far no poem has blossomed such a flower
In Moscow or in Washington.

# The snake and the spider

A poisonous snake
Climbed to the top of the fruit-tree
Made his inability into power
And began to speak compassionately, like a priest.
Blessed are those
Who forgive sharks
Who give their last crumb to the rats
While frogs sing salvation hymns
In their stomachs.

The future
Will heal the mutilation of their souls
Leave them to bathe in happiness.

When the snake made his will law
He mixed sunrays with gases
Set wolves free in parks
Threw dissidents into the sea.

There are things
One may only feel
But never think about.

There are things
One may reflect on
But never express.

There are things
One must neither feel
Think about nor express
And only I know
Why they exist.

And in the happy spirit of a monkey
He murdered all
Who stood in his way.

He then gave alms
Talked about Paradise
Thus all will fall
Who feed on dreams and ideas
Who try to reach up
To the melting ruby of the mirage
Believing illusions can conquer history.

Nearby
A bee struggled
To free itself from cobwebs
Thus all will fall
Who believe in work
And love to fly
Said the spider, without thought or feeling,
While he greedily sucked the honey.

The light turned its face towards night
And died out
The air filled with the smell of death.

# The churchyard

✝ 20 02 26 — 5585 —— victim of a wedding ✝
✝ 49 10 10 — 3988 —— vicitm of divorce ✝
✝ 66 10 26 — 3663 —— victim of brainwashing ✝
✝ 50 04 17 — 8474 —— victim of drugs ✝
✝ 44 09 01 — 6981 —— victim of loneliness ✝
✝ 35 02 08 — 7329 —— victim of orgasm ✝
✝ 39 08 05 — 6224 —— victim of socialism ✝
✝ 25 12 02 — 5275 —— victim of jealousy ✝
✝ 10 10 10 — 3226 —— victim of the gods ✝
✝ 18 02 13 — 3482 —— victim of politics ✝
✝ 22 07 17 — 9484 —— victim of equality ✝
✝ 16 08 18 — 9527 —— victim of kindness ✝
✝ 20 12 08 — 3428 —— victim of boredom ✝
✝ 40 06 16 — 4948 —— victim of justice ✝
✝ 28 05 13 — 8632 —— victim of tax ✝
✝ 38 09 15 — 9516 —— victim of indifference ✝
✝ 45 01 01 — 6558 —— victim of nuclear power ✝
✝ 56 10 14 — 2531 —— victim of poverty ✝
✝ 27 05 15 — 3312 —— victim of wealth ✝
✝ 36 08 22 — 6391 —— victim of lies ✝
✝ 54 12 01 — 3011 —— victim of thieves ✝
✝ 14 06 19 — 2890 —— victim of fascism ✝
✝ 48 04 14 — 7394 —— victim of stalinism ✝
✝ 33 11 22 — 3386 —— victim of car accident ✝
✝ 26 05 23 — 5162 —— victim of work ✝
✝ 39 07 29 — 7228 —— victim of humanism ✝
✝ 20 10 30 — 5072 —— victim of stupidity ✝
✝ 30 02 10 — 9373 —— victim of truth ✝
✝ 64 11 28 — 1974 —— victim of unemployment ✝
✝ 22 03 13 — 6575 —— victim of poetry ✝
✝ 50 04 24 — 1628 —— victim of friendship ✝
✝ 78 06 25 — 2868 —— victim of hunger ✝
✝ 42 07 27 — 3767 —— victim of freedom ✝
✝ 23 08 23 — 5363 —— victim of destruction of environment ✝
✝ 18 10 28 — 2468 —— victim of war ✝
✝ 38 08 18 — 3673 —— victim of children ✝
✝ 56 04 27 — 4275 —— victim of hate ✝
✝ 37 10 10 — 1974 —— victim of voracity ✝

✝ 68 03 06 — 7421 —— victim of school ✝
✝ 52 11 29 — 4673 —— victim of love ✝
✝ 45 05 09 — 5189 —— victim of peace ✝
✝ 22 08 22 — 2648 —— victim of treachery ✝
✝ 33 06 26 — 8532 —— victim of capitalism ✝
✝ 56 03 14 — 9373 —— victim of an air disaster ✝
✝ 16 09 20 — 3363 —— victim of alcohol ✝
✝ 26 05 15 — 5672 —— victim of the victim of other victims ✝

Rest in peace!


# Life after death

Life after death
Does not interest me
I have had enough of this one.

# 6

## Stay in Your Own Skin

# Careful

Be careful at dawn
Leave no traces
The lightning might find you
And strike

Be careful with words
The sun makes mistakes
Each time it believes in the clouds

Be careful with your heart
From hate no trees can grow

Be careful with life
A wolf aware of the lamb's situation
Starves and dies

# Poetry

*To Artur Lundkvist*

Ideologies no longer make war
Class-war snores on the sofa
Today it is the hearts who fight and divorce
Love is called 'click'.
Philosophers pick strawberries in the woods
No one believes in thoughts any more
People carry numbers instead of names.
Poets read poetry in literary pubs
The guests horoscopes in evening papers
And chew gum.
Poetry is useless
Bureaucrats discuss culture
And scratch their arses
Those who aren't pleased can swear.

Freedom
Flies yawning over the world.

# Retraining

Since retraining began
Nobody practices his own profession
Dressmakers no longer make dresses
They discuss the literary universe
And the structural nothingness
Poets in the market-place explain
How to make pins
Lawyers pick bugs from fruit-trees
While killers watch, cigar in mouth
Doctors sweep laziness out of the offices
Spraying them with lily of the valley
The women are in a meeting
Rehabilitated revolutionaries
Live secluded and shy like snails
A painter shouts from the scaffolding:
Gentlemen, the world's not going to change!

# Repetitio mater studiorum est

Maybe everything's been said in the world
But not everything's been heard
So say it once again over and over
In the name of freedom of expression.

Repetitio mater studiorum est.

Pity truth is not a flower
We could recognise it by its scent
And no one need die for it any more
In the name of freedom of expression.

Repetitio mater studiorum est.

All things pass and all is repeated
The wounds of time bleed and hurt
History amputates
In the name of freedom of expression.

Repetitio mater studiorum est.

# Thought and heart

You can't understand people as they are
Unless you disregard yourself
And forget everything you know about them
Like the sun
The thought shines with shadows
And cannot see the goal for its own light.
Two plus two is not always four
Truth lies hidden in an oyster
But how will we find the oysters
When no one can walk twice in the same water
And no oysters can be in two places at once.
We must experience the world with our hearts
Only the heart can feel
What thought cannot see
But without thought
The heart sees people larger than life
Bursts into flames and burns.

# Nothing is changed

Nothing is changed in the world
The apple is still an apple
And the snake a snake
Wheat is the same as always
The stone is a little softer
But still a stone
The word as in the beginning: overwhelming light.
Those who cannot exist themselves
Create those who exist.
Hamlet still seeks the truth
While the mad Ophelia cries.
Love is not a convent
The churches are full of sin
Man cannot be saved.

# History

There have always existed fortifications
That no army could conquer
There have always existed men
That no power could corrupt
But so far there's never been an army
That hasn't been conquered
And no power
That was not crushed.

# Poet

So he is a poet
Said mother-in-law with surprise
And a philosopher, smiled father-in-law
A foreigner
Whispered the neighbours
Poetry is nonsense
You can't make your living by it
My wife reminded me
What do they live on, these poets
Asked the labour exchange
On vitamins
Where do they get them
They pick them
From words
From books
From the air
From the earth
Bark
Shouted the policeman
Poets love to bark at the moon
I don't bark
I only cry like a wolf sometimes.

# Stay in your own skin

Stay in your own skin
With your heart in your head
Or your head in your stomach
But stay
Be obstinate like the stone
Like water and fire unwilling to marry
Like the moon unwilling to fall
Like grass growing against the wish of the wind
Like iron unwilling to rust
Like rust unwilling to be iron
Like a jealous wife
Like the magnetic needle always pointing north
Like God unwilling to show himself
Or to shape the word
After your image.

# The yellow pain of the day

I close my eyes
And the yellow pain of the day has gone

Thought gathers whispers from the dream
And interprets them again and again
Until they wither

The night tears off unsure leaves
And whistles

Owls laugh at the cocks
Who forgot to crow at midnight

Water flows towards loneliness
The moon finds its way to the sea
And sinks

I catch a fleeing star
With a pin
And watch a flower blossom
At the end of the last word

# Summer

Summer is the season
When time gently stretches
Like a woman in love
And no natural law is valid

Angels of honey fly heavily
And sing to the harvest
Things dream satiated with tiredness
Life turns its face towards the sun
Sunning itself

Large bundles of wheat come raining from the sky
But God is asleep and no one understands the wonder

Man must rise when heaven sinks down
And the rainbow changes colour

There is always light in the water
Only people can find it
And adorn it with roses of myth

Summer is the season
When fate ripens
And he who is late
Will never arrive.

# To be is to laugh

Break the lamps of the liars
And laugh.

Don't believe that it is dawn
Because the sun
Caresses your hair.

There are still plains
Where the mist has not risen
Where the brain is directed
Among slipping mountains
Making the promise impossible.

Yet there is hope
Also in a withered flower
In a stone on the road
In the lonely cloud.

The world is green
Filled with butterflies and tears

And to be is to laugh.

# Go there

Go there where the wheat ripens
Go there without wondering
If the night has an end
Without being surprised
When someone with closed eyes
Asks you:
Where is the road?
The goal is always different
When you arrive
Don't scatter dreams in the air
The road is meaningless
If the river does not flow
And you undress
Only those prepared to dive
From the steep cliff
Will find the word that sings.

# Emptiness

People pale with loneliness
Seek nourishment in pharmacies
And are afraid to be glad

Brainwashed children
Looking for their parents at tribunals
Their parents go separate ways
As if enchanted
Souls being chased by material things

Teenagers scream
So they won't go astray
Ideas with fists
In their pockets
Angels selling love on the pavements
Dead snails in the beds

Justice doesn't kill any more
People kill themselves with happiness
They make their history
With family and salary.

# Birds

I woke up one morning
With birds in my head.
'The birds must be caged',
The birdkeeper shouted.
'The birds should fly and sing',
Cried the hunters
Shooting wildly towards the sky.

# There are days

There are days
When one single sunray is enough
And the world is a different colour
Cherry flowers from heaven fall on your lap
Time flows singing within you.

There are days
When it's all dark
When time comes to an end and water stops
The day has no strength to open its eyes
Life abandons its weapons, overcome.

# Love

Throw the words into the fire
Stop the wind
To love is to be quiet and listen to music.

Don't ask the fish why he drinks water
He can swim, that's enough
Believe everything and wait.

Fruit is not always harvested in the autumn
There are also autumns with buds
Time is always the same
Only the hands of the clock move around
And people who pass.

Water your body with the water of love
Otherwise it will wither
And teach the stones to caress each other
Behind the wall
The wedding is still possible
Love is hope that grows in a void.

# Happiness

This morning I woke up unusually happy
Only good news in the papers, on the radio
Lilies in blossom smiling in the garden
Happy children playing games in the street
Blissful birds sing songs about rebirth
The air is fragrant, clean and fresh
The world is at peace with the laws of nature
I touch wood and cry and sing
Life is wonderful and it's great to be alive.

# Love and future

There is no future in love
Only the present exists
People in love lock into happiness.

Now or never!

The story of love
Is a fight against time
Life enclosed
Between two fierce enemies —
Knowledge and eternity.

## Poesia non muori

'Today in this world there are about fifty tons
of explosives per person.
How many milligrams of poetry per head of the
                                                population are there?'
A lieutenant asked me
'We defend life with weapons
Not with rubbish.'

'A football player today costs millions.
How much does a poet cost?'
Asked my accountant
'No loans for poetry,
God only helps those who possess.'

'Happy or unhappy
Man still dies.'
A psychologist comforted me:
'Take your medicine without complaining.
Tempus dolores tua delebit.'

Poesia non muori.

# Romanian Writers
## Published by Forest Books

### AN ANTHOLOGY OF
### CONTEMPORARY ROMANIAN POETRY

Translated by Andrea Deletant and Brenda Walker

A selection of work by poets, including world-famous writers such as Marin Sorescu and Nina Cassian, writing under the difficult conditions of the Ceausescu dictatorship.

ISBN 0 950948 74 8                    112 pages/£6.95

### PIED POETS
### CONTEMPORARY VERSE OF THE
### TRANSYLVANIAN AND DANUBE GERMANS
### OF ROMANIA

Selected and Translated by Robert Elsie

Poetry by the German minority living in Romania, many of whom fled the Ceausescu regime.

ISBN 0 948259 77 9                    208 pages/£8.95

### VLAD DRACULA
### THE IMPALER

*A play by*
*Marin Sorescu*

Translated by Dennis Deletant

This play by Marin Sorescu shows a ravaged land — a world full of whispers and spies; injustice and despair, where suspicion is rife. Is its ruler a martyr or a madman?

ISBN 0 948259 07 8                    112 pages/£6.95

## The Thirst of
## The Salt Mountain

*A trilogy of plays by*
*Marin Sorescu*

Translated by Andrea Deletant and Brenda Walker

Marin Sorescu, one of Romania's most controversial poets and playwrights, has both the philosophic depth of Beckett and his own very special vision about the impossibility of communication in everyday life. Beckett's god is dead, Sorescu's only tired.

ISBN 0 9509487 5 6                                            124 pages/£6.95

## *Stories and Poems from Scandinavia*
## *Published by Forest Books*

### Snow and Summers

*by Solveig von Schoultz*

Translated by Anne Born

Winner of numerous literary prizes, Solveig von Schoultz is widely acknowledged as one of Finland's leading poets and prose writers. This volume presents the cream of her poetry from almost fifty years for the first time in England. 'For both poet and reader von Schoultz's poetry is an exercise in the sharpening of vision . . . sincerity and smiling wisdom engendered by a lifetime of experience.' *(Bo Carpelan)*

ISBN 0 948259 52 3                                            112 pages/£7.95

## Heartwork

*by Solveig von Schoultz*

'Her stories present an acute and subtle analysis of human relationships. She is not only a listener and an observer: she is also passionately involved with these dramas of everyday life which are all concerned with the problems of human value and human growth. These she portrays without sentimentality but with the rich perception of experience.' *(Bo Carpelan)*

ISBN 0 948259 50 7                    144 pages/£7.95

## Preparations for Flight & Other Swedish Stories

Translated by Robin Fulton

Robin Fulton, one of the best-known translators of contemporary Swedish literature, has gathered a collection of stories which, as he says in his preface, remained in his mind long after a first reading. In all of them, concrete reality evokes mystery, and in many of them, childhood recollections affect and are affected by everyday adult experience.

ISBN 0 948259 66 3                    176 pages/£8.95